D1524587

Reading & Writing

The Revolution
of the
Alphabet

Reading & Writing

The Revolution
of the
Alphabet

WITHDRAWN

Marshall Cavendish
Benchmark
New York

This edition first published in 2009 in North America by Marshall Cavendish Benchmark.

Marshall Cavendish Benchmark
99 White Plains Road
Tarrytown, NY 10591
www.marshallcavendish.us

Library of Congress Cataloging-in-Publication Data

Rossi, Renzo, 1940–
   The revolution of the alphabet / by Renzo Rossi.
      p. cm. — (Reading and writing)
   ISBN 978-0-7614-4320-9
   1. Writing–History–Juvenile literature. 2. Alphabet–History–Juvenile literature. I. Title.
   P211.R672 2009
   411.09—dc22
                              2008032289

Text: Renzo Rossi
Editing: Cristiana Leoni
Translation: Erika Pauli
Design and layout: Luigi Ieracitano
Illustrations: Alessandro Baldanzi, Lorenzo Cecchi, Sauro Giampaia, Luigi Ieracitano, Paola Ravaglia, Donato Spedaliere, Roberto Simoni, Studio Stalio
Maps: Roberto Simoni

Photographs: Scala Archives pp. 12, 18, 19, 20, 23, 29

Printed in Malaysia
1 3 5 6 4 2

Contents

Toward an Alphabet

One of the first things we learn at school is the alphabet: a series of signs, each of which has a single sound, that we join together to form the words of the language we speak.

Even though this system seems so simple, it is one of the greatest inventions of humankind. The oldest systems of writing used drawings to stand for words. Not surprisingly, they needed many different signs. The alphabet, however, is composed of just a few letters, and by arranging them in different ways we can write an enormous number of words.

This makes writing easy and it is why so many people eventually adopted the alphabet, gradually adapting it to the phonetic requirements of their languages.

Opposite, top to bottom:

The Greek word for "puppies"

The entrance sign to the Museum of Israel in Jerusalem is written in both English and Hebrew.

The masthead of an Arab newspaper

The Cyrillic alphabet is used in Russia and part of eastern Europe.

Below: Several European languages use Latin characters like the ones below.

Νεογέννητα

العربي القدس

AL-QUDS AL-ARABI

يومية ـ سياسية ـ مستقلة

ФИНИНСПЕКТОРОМ

,

ие, имею

...мещался парад

...жно было через сени; к

...адное крыльцо, за свою красоту

...аличие сеней типично для

...тия. Святые сени пред

...ение, перекрыто

...этажом раз

...й.

A Phoenician Invention

The alphabet was invented at least 3,500 years ago by the Phoenicians, skillful merchants and formidable navigators who lived in what is now Lebanon. It may have been invented by just one person. If it was, he must have been a real genius who was familiar with the writings of the other Mediterranean peoples. Guided by these, he created something completely new and original: a phonetic alphabet, or an alphabet based on the sounds of the spoken language. Phoenician writing is read from right to left.

Below: Phoenician ships head toward Mediterranean ports. Thanks to their activities as merchants, the Phoenicians spread their alphabet wherever they traded.

Above: A carving from the 8th century BCE of Phoenician ships transporting tree trunks.

Opposite, bottom: A map of the Mediterranean during the time of the Phoenicians.

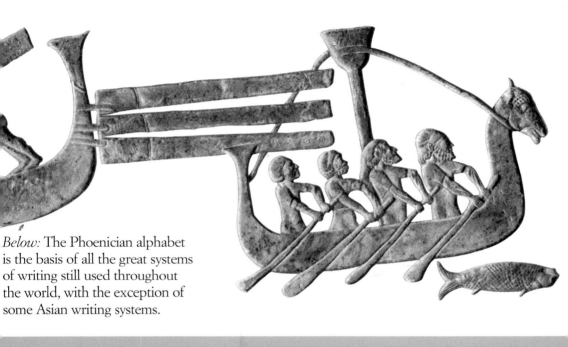

Below: The Phoenician alphabet is the basis of all the great systems of writing still used throughout the world, with the exception of some Asian writing systems.

| a | b | c,g | d | e | f | h | i,j | k | l | m |
| n | o | p | q | r | s | t | u,v,w | x | z | |

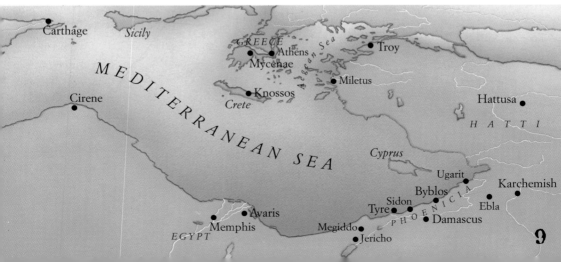

Carthage *Sicily*

GREECE
Athens
Mycenae *Aegean Sea* Troy

Miletus

M E D I T E R R A N E A N   S E A

Cirene

Knossos
Crete

Hattusa

H A T T I

Cyprus

Ugarit
Karchemish

Byblos
Sidon *P H O E N I C I A* Ebla
Tyre Damascus

Avaris
Memphis Megiddo
EGYPT Jericho

Hebrew Writing

The Jews, who lived in the Middle East, used a script derived from Phoenician script to write the first books of the Bible—the Torah—which are sacred texts of their religion.

They later adopted Aramaic script, which was widespread throughout the Near East for commercial and diplomatic contacts, and used it to write some of the books of the Bible. Today it is used as a literary and religious script.

Finally the Jews worked out what is known as Square Hebrew script, so-called because of the regularity of the letters. A slightly modified version is still in use in Israel. The alphabet has 22 consonants and the vowels are indicated with dots or lines located above or below the consonants.

Below: When this coin was made in the 1st century BCE in Palestine, the Hebrew characters had already existed for more than 600 years.

Left: This Aramaic inscription from the 9th century BCE represents the first time in the history of writing that words are divided by spaces.

10

Above: Script from a Dead Sea scroll.

Below: Members of the Essenes, a Jewish religious group, copy the sacred texts of the Hebrew religion. Some of these documents were found in 1947 in the Qumran caves, near the Dead Sea. This is why they are known as the Dead Sea Scrolls.

Left: The consonant *d* is associated with various vowels, represented by the dots, in Hebrew script.

di   do   du

A Greek Contribution

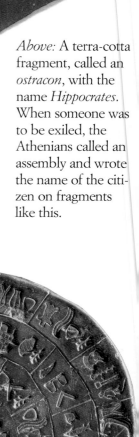

According to Herodotus, the great Greek historian who lived in the 5th century BCE, a Phoenician named Cadmus introduced writing to the Greeks.

The Greeks did indeed learn the alphabet from the Phoenicians, but they added a few important innovations. The Greek language is particularly rich in vowels (for example, there were two different types of "e"), which had to be clearly indicated. Some of the Phoenician consonant signs had sounds that did not exist in spoken Greek, so the Greeks used those signs for their vowels. Thus, for the first time in the history of writing, vowels appeared around the 8th century BCE.

Above: A terra-cotta fragment, called an *ostracon*, with the name *Hippocrates*. When someone was to be exiled, the Athenians called an assembly and wrote the name of the citizen on fragments like this.

Many centuries earlier, the peoples who inhabited Greece and islands in the Aegean Sea used difficult systems of writing similar to Egyptian hieroglyphs.

Right: The Phaestos Disk, from Crete, dates to the 12th century BCE. It has an inscription in hieroglyphic signs that begins at the edge and moves in a spiral to the center.

12

α	alpha	ι	iota	ρ	rho	
β	beta	κ	kappa	σ	sigma	
γ	gamma	λ	lambda	τ	tau	
δ	delta	μ	mu	υ	upsilon	
ε	epsilon	ν	nu	φ	phi	
ζ	zeta	ξ	xi	χ	chi	
η	eta	ο	omicron	ψ	psi	
θ	theta	π	pi	ω	omega	

Left: The lower case letters of the Greek alphabet. The term *alphabet*, coined in the 3rd century CE, is derived from the first two Greek letters: alpha and beta.

Left: The image of this Greek scholar writing on a tablet was depicted on a vase. Greeks covered their writing tablets with wax and etched letters into the soft surface.

Below: A Greek inscription from the 7th century BCE closely resembles letters in the Phoenician alphabet. It is composed of five names in four rows; the first and the fourth are read from right to left, the second and the third from left to right.

13

Poets and Philosophers

The Greek alphabet was adopted by all the regions in continental Greece and the colonies.

The Greeks wrote many works of literature still read today. Even younger readers know of the feats of Achilles and Ulysses, the unforgettable heroes of Homer's poems, the *Iliad* and the *Odyssey*, written in the 8th century BCE. Thereafter, masters such as Aristotle, Sophocles, and Aeschylus wrote philosophical texts and composed plays for the theater.

The laws were also put down in writing to guarantee the same justice to all; the wealthy and powerful could no longer interpret the laws according to their whims.

Left: Aristotle was one of greatest classical Greek thinkers. He founded a school called the Lyceum in Athens. His works are still well-respected.

Opposite: A Greek theater had tiers for the spectators arranged in a semicircle around the stage. The theater became an art center in the 5th century BCE with the plays of Aeschylus, Sophocles, Euripedes, and Aristophanes.

Theater masks were used by the Greek actors to represent comic (*right*) and tragic (*left*) characters. They also served as sound boxes to amplify the actors' voices.

15

The Greatest Library

Even after Greece lost its liberty to Rome, Greek culture continued to dominate the Western world. In the 3rd century BCE a great complex was built in Alexandria, Egypt. It included collections of art, an astronomical observatory, and even a zoological garden. Most important were the two libraries that housed 700,000 books covering all fields of knowledge. It was known as the Museum (house of the muses) after the Greek goddesses who protected all the intellectual and artistic activities of mankind.

The Museum was a real research center, much like our universities, where the greatest minds of the time could freely devote themselves to study, experimentation, literature, history, and the sciences.

The library, which was in use for three centuries, was almost completely destroyed by fire in 47 BCE.

Left, top: A coin with the effigy of Alexander the Great and a Greek inscription proclaiming him king of the Macedonians. He conquered far-flung lands over which he spread Greek culture. In Egypt he founded the city of Alexandria.

Facing page: The great Library of Alexandria was founded by Ptolemy I, who governed Egypt after the death of Alexander.

Left: To make research easier, tags with the titles of the works were attached to the ends of the papyrus rolls stacked on the shelves.

An Etruscan Mystery

Historians are still unable to pinpoint the origin of the Etruscans, a people who lived in central northern Italy side by side with the Latins (ancestors of the Romans) and other peoples of ancient Italy.

The Etruscans traded with the Greeks, who had colonies in southern Italy. They learned the alphabet from them and adapted it to the Etruscan language. The Etruscan alphabet has 21 consonants and 5 vowels. It not only provided the basis of the Latin alphabet, but also spread to other Italian peoples who modified it for their own languages.

The Etruscan alphabet has been deciphered and we can read the words, but, since our knowledge of the language is very poor, we are unable to understand the meaning of Etruscan texts.

Right: A serpent decorated with an Etruscan inscription coils around this small perfume jar.

Above: The letters on the upper border of this ivory tablet, made in the 8th century BCE, run from right to left. Pupils used these letters as models for their writing exercises.

Above and right: A small vessel in the shape of a rooster from Viterbo, a powerful Etruscan city. It is in *bucchero*, a shiny black ceramic invented by the Etruscans. The complete alphabet is etched on it.

The Latin Alphabet

When the Etruscan civilization was at its zenith, Rome was still not much more than a village of shepherds. The Etruscans exercised an early political and cultural influence on Rome, and it is easy to understand why the Romans adopted the Etruscan alphabet to write Latin, their own language. But since the languages are different, a few changes had to be made. Latin had some sounds that did not exist in Etruscan, so the Romans borrowed a few letters—including X, Y, and Z—from the Greek alphabet.

To carve inscriptions on stone, the Romans worked out a type of writing—majuscule—that used capital letters. Offshoots of this were the rustic capitals, which were narrower and had less regular lines, and cursive script, for daily use.

Not until much later did the minuscule, or lower case, script evolve from a gradual simplification of uncial script, which combined rounded majuscules with some cursive forms.

Above: "Beware of the dog" was written at the entrances of many Roman houses.

Below: There is a distinct difference between capital script (*top*) and rustic script (*bottom*).

Opposite, below: Cursive capital and uncial script. Uncial spread throughout the regions of the Roman Empire where Latin was written.

To carve the inscriptions on stone, a Roman stone cutter traced lines on the slab to make sure the letters would be straight. In addition to a chisel and hammer, he used a square, a compass, and a plumb line.

Tools for Writing

Originally the Romans wrote on the leaves and bark of trees. Later they used waxed tablets or linen cloth. Not until the 2nd century BCE did the papyrus used to make books arrive from Egypt. Papyrus scrolls were usually written on one side only. Each end of the papyrus was glued to a stick so the scroll, known as a *volumen* by the Romans, could be held. Readers had to be careful that the entire scroll didn't unroll.

Parchment reached Rome much later. It was invented in the city of Pergamum, in what is now Turkey. Parchment is made from lamb- or sheepskin, worked so that it becomes smooth and thin. But this material was never commonly used because it was too expensive. A quill or reed pen dipped in ink was used to write on both papyrus and parchment.

Above: A container for storing papyrus scrolls

Below: Like the Greeks and the Etruscans, Roman children learned to write on waxed tablets, which were often joined together like a modern notebook. Letters were written with the pointed end of the stylus and errors were erased with the spatula end.

Above: The young woman in this painting is holding a stylus and waxed tablets.

Left: Two styluses, each with one pointed end and one spatula-shaped end, and a reed pen called a *calmus*. The pen would be dipped into ink made from soot or squid ink.

23

Letters of the Prophet

Arab writing, like Hebrew writing, is derived from Aramaic and appears on coins and inscriptions of the nomad Arab populations of northern Arabia beginning in the 2nd century BCE. The Romans called these groups Nabataeans. Nabataean writing later became the Arab script of Islam, the religion founded by the prophet Muhammed in 622 CE.

Two types of writing developed simultaneously: the Kufic (from Kufa, a Mesopotamian center of Arab culture) for use on monuments, and the Naskhi ("of the manuscript") for books and normal writing. Both use 29 signs and are read from right to left.

Left: One of the 99 names of Allah is written in Arabic on this square tile.

Opposite: Young Muslim students study the Koran, the holy book of Islam, under the guidance of their teacher.

Right: This bronze hand is inscribed with ancient Arabic writing.

بِسْمِ اللّٰهِ الرَّحْمٰنِ

Left and above: Kufic script is geometric with many open corners that face upward (*left*). The curved, rounded forms of Naskhi script are interconnected (*above*).

Fantastic Forms

The true originality of Arab writing is its capacity to assume countless forms and to lend itself to prodigious transformations. The importance of the script is derived from the fact that it must communicate the word of Allah. This is why calligraphy (which means "beautiful script") is Islamic art, by definition one of the two koranic arts. The other is the recitation of Islam's holy book, the Koran. It thus became the essential decorative element of the mosques and all other Islamic monuments.

Arab calligraphy has undergone an infinite variety of style changes and has achieved a high level of elegance and expressiveness.

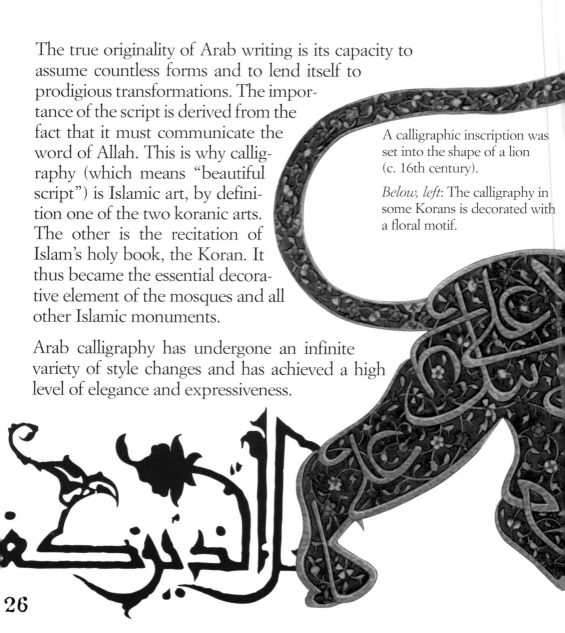

A calligraphic inscription was set into the shape of a lion (c. 16th century).

Below, left: The calligraphy in some Korans is decorated with a floral motif.

26

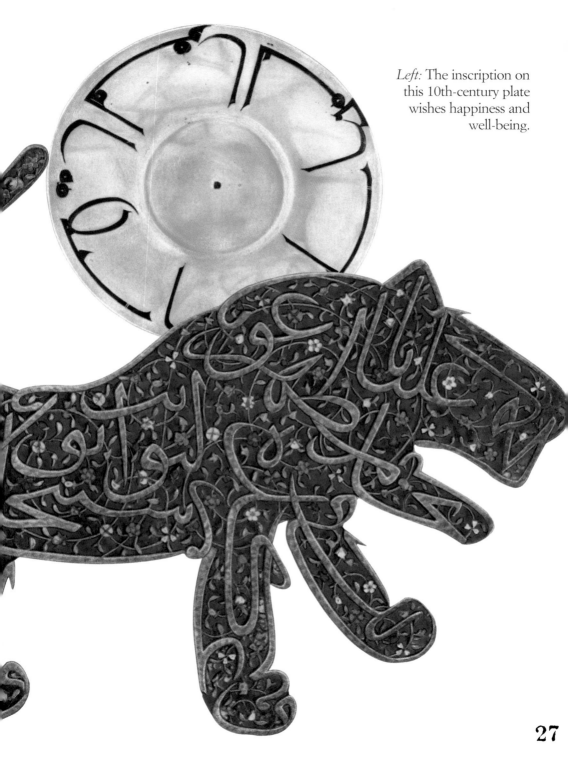

Left: The inscription on this 10th-century plate wishes happiness and well-being.

In India

Ancient Indian writings represent the most important offspring of the Phoenician-derived Aramaic script, which reached northern India from Mesopotamia around 800 BCE, giving birth to the Brahmi and the Kharosthi scripts. The latter disappeared in the 5th century CE, but Brahmi remained vital and led to an infinite variety of styles of writing, not only in India but also in the Far East.

One of these, which became popular in the 7th century, was Nagari ("civic") script. A modified version of Nagari script, called Devanagari ("nagari of the gods"), is still used today.

Devanagari script is composed of syllables. The consonants and vowels are bound together by a horizontal bar to form a single graphic sign that represents a spoken sound.

In present-day India 19 different scripts are used to write the 15 official languages.

Below: Even though they are oriented differently, the resemblance between Phoenician letters (*left*) and Indian (*right*) letters is striking.

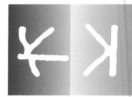

Left: The horizontal bar that connects the syllables of a word in Devanagari script is called a ligature.

त्यवक्षारान्तृपः पश्येदिद्धद्धिर्ब्राह्मणैः सत्र ।
धर्मशास्त्रानुसारेण क्रोधलोभविवर्जितः ॥ १ ॥

Right: An Indian scribe writing on strips of dried smoothed palm. They are held together by cords and form a "book" that opens accordian-style.

Above: This illustrated page is from the *Kalpa-sutra*, an Indian text that contains the rules for religious ceremonies.

29

Index

Page numbers in **boldface** are illustrations, tables, and charts.